B*LL*CKS

PREVIOUS BOOKS BY MICHAEL EATON

The Priest of Nemi, Shoestring Press, 2013
Head Hunters, Shoestring Press, 2015
Based On A True Story, Shoestring Press, 2020 (reprinted 2023)

B*LL*CKS

A Word On Trial

MICHAEL EATON

All rights reserved. No part of this work covered by the copyright herein may be reproduced or used in any means – graphic, electronic, or mechanical, including copying, recording, taping, or information storage and retrieval systems – without written permission of the publisher.

Printed by imprintdigital
Upton Pyne, Exeter
www.digital.imprint.co.uk

Typesetting by The Book Typesetters
hello@thebooktypesetters.com
07422 598 168
www.thebooktypesetters.com

Published by Shoestring Press
19 Devonshire Avenue, Beeston, Nottingham, NG9 1BS
(0115) 925 1827
www.shoestringpress.co.uk

First published 2023
© Copyright: Michael Eaton
© Cover design and illustrations on pp. 1, 25 and 74: Linus Eaton Wattenberg

The moral right of the author has been asserted.

ISBN 978-1-915553-45-4

To Caroline Coon, artist, pioneer and tireless campaigner for Truth and Justice who, on a chill Nottingham November morning, characteristically refused to be bamboozled by ignorant misogynist prosecution. With affection and respect.

BOLLOCKS!

There are two Narrators: The STORY-TELLER *is a crabby down-to-earth chap in his 60s, a Nottingham man, and this local story means so much to him. The* COMMENTATOR *is an uppity younger female academic who wishes to make some cultural sense of an ancient history. They are frequently and axiomatically at odds with one another as they set the scene and comment on the action, forever vying to take control of the narrative.*

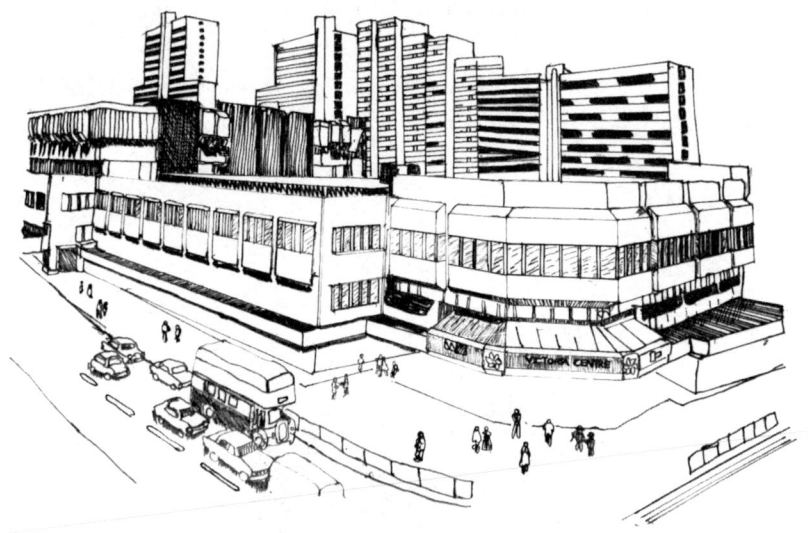

STORY-TELLER: Nottingham, my home town…

COMMENTATOR: Every story needs a Location…

STORY-TELLER: In 1977, the year of the Silver Jubilee…

COMMENTATOR: Every story needs a Beginning…

STORY-TELLER: Fallen leaves off the sooty trees around Old Market Square squelching underfoot. Snot-nosed kids mugging indifferent pedestrians: Penny for the Guy. Not that a copper coin of the realm would have bought many Bangers, Jumping Jacks or Catherine Wheels in those inflationary times.

	Now the national scapegoat on the collective Bonfire Night pyre is Johnny Rotten.
COMMENTATOR:	This is what sociologists would call a Moral Panic…

He can't hide his scorn:

STORY-TELLER:	This is what my generation – who were around at the time – would call an Establishment stitch-up. You weren't even born!
COMMENTATOR:	I'm well aware of the historical significance of The Sex Pistols…

Back in time to 1977.

FADE TO:

EXT. VIRGIN RECORDS, NOTTINGHAM 1977. DAY.

'Progressive' Krautrock music spills out of the door of Virgin Records on King Street, Nottingham: The Faust Tapes.

STORY-TELLER:	A young WPC, Julie Dawn Storey, is patrolling her city-centre beat on that misty autumnal Saturday morning when she is shocked, outraged, to see an album sleeve displayed in the window of the Virgin Records store on King Street.

WPC JULIE STOREY, *in her early 20s, goes inside to confront* CHRIS SEALE, *the young man behind the counter.*

2

CUT TO:

INT. VIRGIN RECORDS, NOTTINGHAM. DAY.

WPC STOREY: Who's in charge here?

CHRIS SEALE: You're speaking to him.

WPC STOREY: You don't look old enough to be the Manager.

CHRIS SEALE: You don't look old enough to be a police officer.

The Story-Teller interrupts as he will throughout:

STORY-TELLER: Chris Seale is twenty-five, bewhiskered, bejumpered, ex-public school – very much in the mould of the founder of the Virgin enterprise, Richard Branson.

The Commentator interrupts as she will throughout:

COMMENTATOR: Later <u>Sir</u> Richard Branson.

WPC STOREY: I'm sure you must know why I'm here.

Chris is genuinely nonplussed:

CHRIS SEALE: Why don't you give us a clue?

WPC STOREY: It's not obscured in any way!

CHRIS SEALE: What?

WPC STOREY: On that record sleeve in your window… The Word!

CHRIS SEALE: What Word?

WPC STOREY: You don't expect me to say it, do you?

The penny drops:

CHRIS SEALE: Oh, The Sex Pistols album?

WPC STOREY: I'm horrified… I'm disgusted… to see such a Word on open display to the citizens of the Queen of the Midlands.

CHRIS SEALE: Has anybody complained?

WPC STOREY: That's beside the point. What's your name, sir?

She takes out her notebook officially. Chris is unable not to sneer:

CHRIS SEALE: Christopher Seale.

WPC STOREY: Well, Mister Seale, I'm asking you to take that offensive item out of the window.

Chris is amazed:

CHRIS SEALE: What about freedom of speech?

WPC STOREY: Are you telling me you're refusing to comply with a reasonable request?

CHRIS SEALE: I haven't heard one yet.

WPC STOREY: I'll be back… and next time I won't be alone.

She stomps out and Chris calls after her:

CHRIS SEALE: What law have we broken?

At this she seems really flummoxed:

WPC STOREY: You'll soon find out.

DISSOLVE.

STORY-TELLER:	Remember, remember the Fifth of November.
	Remember this country in the 1970s?
	The headline in the local rag said it all…

A wheezy old Evening Post SELLER *of the 70s calls out:*

NEWS SELLER:	Late Post. Late Post. Days of Strife in Notts. Late Post.

STORY-TELLER:	Miners pressing for a ballot to determine whether they would go out on strike again. A series of one-day stoppages and an overtime ban bringing the production line at Raleigh Cycle Factory to a halt as employees seek a pay hike. Unofficial walk-outs at the Stanton and Staveley Ironworks.

5

A ragbag 'Dad's Army' of volunteers formed as Fire-fighters back a call to work to rule… though they give an assurance that they would come out to free anyone who found themselves stuck in a lift – not an impossible outcome as workers in local power stations mount a series of wildcat strikes leading to frequent unpredictable electrical shut-downs. Hospitals gear up for an epidemic… of Whooping Cough. Widespread chaos as seventy-five miles per hour winds cause havoc and devastation on the county's roads.

And, according to a shock report from the Ministry of Agriculture, Nottinghamshire is found to be the worst county in England for rodent infestation. Rats!

Despite the protests of a few out-numbered liberal social workers, County Councillors voted to reintroduce caning in children's homes:

A forthright female COUNCILLOR *of the time*:

COUNCILLOR: The only discipline that works for some of these delinquents.

STORY-TELLER: In *Kid's Korner*, thirteen-year-old schoolgirl, Angela of Stapleford, memorably summed up the local mood:

ANGELA: This is my poem: *Power Cuts*.
I look around me, what do I see
Unhappy people miserable as can be
They have to sit in the candle glow
How long will these power cuts last?
I don't know
No television, no light
Very dark and boring every night
From four until seven
From seven to eleven
Supposing the lights went out for ever?
Some would not be able to cook
Others could not get warm
What about people in hospitals
What about babies being born?

I'm finding it hard to write this poem,
When will the light come on?
We have no way of knowing.

STORY-TELLER: You'll be glad to hear it was not all doom and gloom. On the culinary front, having opened a store in the brand-new Broad Marsh shopping centre, Pork Farms sell three thousand sausage rolls, even more pasties and pies and no less than seventeen thousand filled cobs in the very first week.

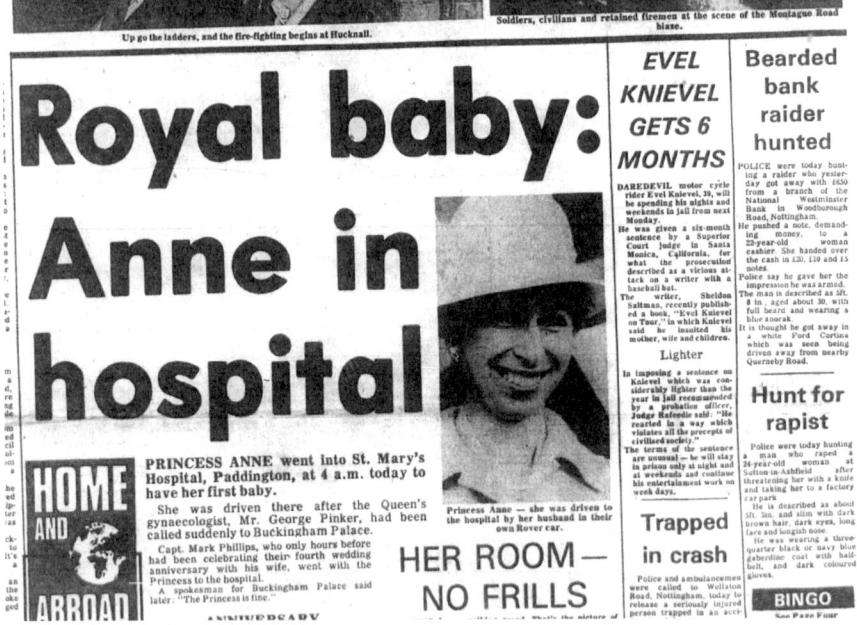

Royal Stop Press: The nation unites in congratulating a 'delighted' Princess Anne who has given birth to a Jubilee baby boy. Gawd bless 'em.

Arriving by coach and horses at Co-Op House on Parliament Street at 11 a.m. approx. Santa would be returning to his Grotto with gendered seasonal largesse: *Formula 500 Racing Set* for the little lads; *Tiny Tears* dolls for the little ladies.

Entertainment News! At the Playhouse: *Much Ado About Nothing* – appropriate motto for the forthcoming affair. On the telly: A choice of evening's viewing. Settling down in front of Saturday night TV there was *The Generation Game* on BBC or you could turn always over to catch N*ew Faces* on ATV in the Midlands.

In the pictures: The Classic Cinema on Market Street was showing X-rated S*winging Wives.* Or at the Savoy you could see *Exorcist Two. The Heretic* – though only at your peril. For just across the county line, Ilkeston magistrates heard the case of an evidently disturbed eighteen-year-old who had been arrested following a shoplifting spree. She offered the entirely plausible justification that the balance of her mind had been disturbed ever since being subjected to *The Exorcist*…

COMMENTATOR: The soundtrack of which was Mike Oldfield's *Tubular Bells*: Virgin Records' first release in 1973 which became an international best-seller and the foundation of Richard Branson's empire…

STORY-TELLER: This distressed lass now claimed to be terrified of the dark and had twice attempted self-harm.

COMMENTATOR: The Derbyshire bench accepted her plea of mitigation and granted a conditional discharge.

STORY-TELLER: In the charts, pop-pickers: Nordic Eurovision winners Abba, much loved by the young yet-to-be Sid Vicious, ruled the roost at Number One with *The Name of the Game*. And entering that week at the bottom of the Top Fifty: novelty platter by the Brighouse and Rastrick Brass Band: *The Floral Dance*.

NEWS SELLER: Late Post! Late post. DJ Jim Arrives For Jubilee Jaunt.

STORY-TELLER: A grainy photograph depicts a much-loved National Treasure with a bleached-blonde barnet and decked-out in an outrageous Union Jack shell suit, gurning characteristically as he pats the head of a young pupil of the Rosehill School on Saint Matthias Road, while the Headmistress, adopting a rictus grin, looks on as if overwhelmed at the great honour of this visitation. This patriotic weirdo has dropped in to spread celebrity joy before engaging on one of his lauded charitable ventures: a sponsored walk for the local Psychiatric Hospital.

COMMENTATOR: *(shocked)* No? You don't mean! Not… Even I have heard of…

STORY-TELLER: How's about that, guys and gals? I told you: You had to have been there.

Unemployment had not yet reached the heights, or depths, of the desperate years to come but recruitment drives were all over the city.
For the Army:

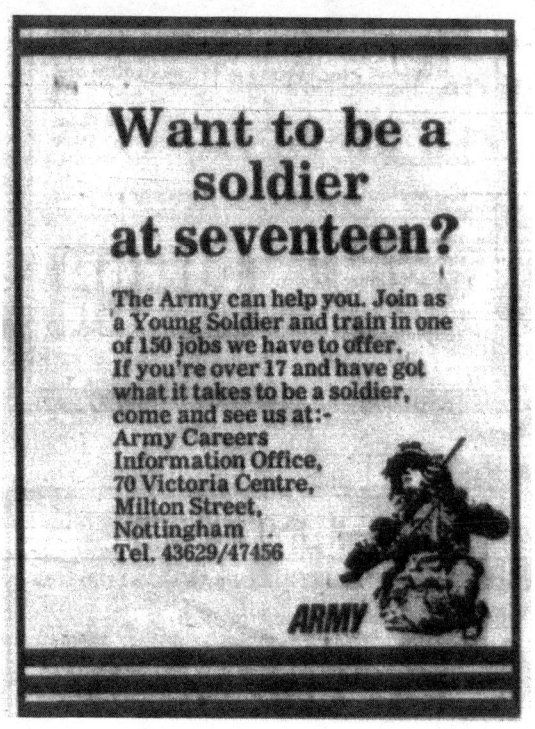

ARMY:	Want to be a Soldier at Seventeen?
STORY-TELLER:	For an even tougher force:
MARINES:	Find out if you could be a Royal Marine Commando.
STORY-TELLER:	And now for something completely different:
AIR FORCE:	The Royal Air Force offers a variety of demanding and rewarding jobs available for men <u>and women</u>.
STORY-TELLER:	Or for such youths who might wish to exert authority nearer home: For the Nottinghamshire Constabulary.

Find out if you could become a Commando.

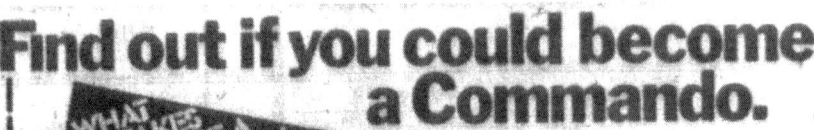

What does it take to become a Royal Marines Commando? How tough is the training? Can you learn a trade? Will you travel?

The answers to all these questions are in our free colour booklet. For your copy, and for more information, call in and have a chat without obligation at the address below.

**R.N. and R.M. Careers Office
70 Milton St., Victoria Centre,
Nottingham NG1 3QX
Tel. Nottingham 49503**

RM ROYAL MARINES COMMANDOS

Top technician training

A Royal Navy engineering apprenticeship means the very finest training, a secure career as one of our top technicians and over £4,000 a year when qualified. Entrants must be between 16-21; and either pass a Navy exam, or have 'O' levels (Grade C or above) or CSE (1), or equivalent, in Maths, English and a physics-based Science.

For a free booklet, and for more information about our Technician Apprenticeship, call in and have a chat without obligation at the address below.

**R.N. and R.M. Careers Office
70 Milton St., Victoria Centre,
Nottingham NG1 3QX
Tel. Nottingham 49503**

You won't find a better Technician Apprenticeship.

RN ROYAL NAVY

AND NOW FOR SOMETHING COMPLETELY DIFFERENT
THE ROYAL AIR FORCE

The Royal Air Force offers you a completely different way of life at work and at play. There are a variety of demanding and rewarding jobs available to men and women, some of which require educational qualifications but many which require only a particular aptitude. We can test your aptitude and, if successful, fully train you for your chosen trade. And life doesn't end after work in the RAF. On most units you will find a whole range of clubs, sports and pastimes.

Sounds interesting? Why not come along to the address below for an informal chat (or write or phone). There is absolutely NO OBLIGATION. It could be the start of something completely different!

RAF CAREERS INFORMATION OFFICE, 70 VICTORIA CENTRE, MILTON STREET, NOTTINGHAM 46407

It could even be WPC STOREY *fronting the recruitment drive:*

POLICE: The Police want you. Are you ready for us?

COMMENTATOR: So that was Nottingham in November 1977?

STORY-TELLER: England's Dreaming. Now you know why we needed The Sex Pistols.

DISSOLVE.

INT. VIRGIN RECORDS NOTTINGHAM. DAY.

More avant-garde European music from a Virgin Records release: Phaedra *by Tangerine Dream.*

STORY-TELLER: After that first visit from the County's Finest…

COMMENTATOR: Nine days after the release of *Never Mind The Bollocks*.

STORY-TELLER: Seale gets straight on the blower to the Boss.

Above the racket Chris talks into the shop's phone:

CHRIS SEALE: It's Chris from the Nottingham store… Can you put me through to Mister Branson?

The cheery well-bred voice of RICHARD BRANSON *comes on the line – he sounds as if everything to him is a wizard wheeze.*

BRANSON: Hi, Chris. Call me Richard. How's sales in Notts?

CHRIS SEALE: Flying out of the bins, Richard, as it happens. But…

BRANSON: Numbers?

CHRIS SEALE: Seven hundred plus and counting. But…

BRANSON: Competition?

14

CHRIS SEALE: We've pretty much got the monopoly. Banned by W.H. Smug. But…

BRANSON: Great! No surprise there.

CHRIS SEALE: Woolworth's refuse to stock it. But…

BRANSON: Have to stick with the Pick 'n Mix then.

CHRIS SEALE: Boots have refused to handle it. But…

BRANSON: Can't even get it on prescription, eh? Great work, Chris.

CHRIS SEALE: But…

BRANSON: We don't do 'buts', Chris.

CHRIS SEALE: But, there's a problem… I had a copper round. She says we have to remove the album cover from public view.

Branson ponders – then chuckles:

BRANSON: Okay… Here's what we do… Take down all other Virgin product…

Chris is surprised at this suggestion:

CHRIS SEALE: The Faust Tapes? Tangerine Dream? Gong? Henry Cow? Even Tubular Bells?

BRANSON: Plaster the entire window with The Sex Pistols record. Like I did at our flagship store.

CHRIS SEALE: But… this is Nottingham, not Notting Hill.

BRANSON: We'll send you a giant poster… And don't play any other records. Blast it out!

CHRIS SEALE: Truth be told, Richard, I can't stand that racket.

BRANSON: Chris… Chris… That's what I thought at first. I'd never heard anything like *Anarchy In the UK.*

CHRIS SEALE: Nor me either. I joined Virgin because I thought you were committed to releasing intelligent sounds by progressive musicians.

BRANSON: Gotcha. But how do you think we're going to subsidise that? We're not the Arts Council, are we? And we can all change our minds, can't we?

CHRIS SEALE: The cop said they'll be back.

BRANSON: Terrific! That's the general idea.

CHRIS SEALE: Couldn't I just take the album out of the window?

BRANSON: You don't want to do that, do you, Chris? Provocation. That's what Punk's all about.

CHRIS SEALE: We're punks now, are we?

BRANSON: This is a question of freedom of speech.

CHRIS SEALE: That's what I said.

BRANSON: What law are we breaking?

CHRIS SEALE: That's what I asked.

BRANSON: Keep shifting those units, my man.

CUT TO:

EXT. VIRGIN STORE. DAY.

This time it's not Prog but Punk – Pretty Vacant *by The Sex Pistols – blaring out as* SERGEANT RAYMOND STONE *and WPC Storey approach the store.*

COMMENTATOR: A couple of days later, true to her word, WPC Storey pays a return visit – this time accompanied by Sergeant Raymond Stone.

STORY-TELLER: Branson's instructions have been carried out to the letter.

Julie Storey is even more outraged than before:

WPC STOREY: What d'you call this, Sarge? There was only one of them on Saturday.

SERGEANT STONE: Don't get yourself in a lather, Julie. Let's see what he has to say for hisself.

CUT TO:

INT. VIRGIN STORE. DAY.

They go inside to confront Chris.

SERGEANT STONE: Mister Seale, you already met my colleague.

WPC STOREY: I told you I'd be back.

At first the Sergeant attempts to be conciliatory:

SERGEANT STONE: Now look here, lad… nobody's trying to stop you selling the record.

But there's a new-found fire in Chris.

CHRIS SEALE: That would hardly be a sound business decision, would it? *Never Mind The Bollocks* is the Number One album in the UK.

WPC STOREY: Not on the BBC charts. Even Melody Maker blacked out that B-word.

CHRIS SEALE: Cowards.

SERGEANT STONE: All we're asking is for some co-operation.

WPC STOREY: Thirty-two record sleeves in the window… I counted. And that poster: nine foot by six on my reckoning. A deliberate affront. This is King Street, Nottingham, not King's Road, Chelsea.

SERGEANT STONE: Tell you what we do, Chris: Remove the records, flog them under the counter in a brown paper bag and we'll say no more about it.

CHRIS SEALE: Not an option, I'm afraid.

SERGEANT STONE: Who's ordering you to do this?

CHRIS SEALE: Who's ordering <u>you?</u>

The Sergeant makes one last attempt:

SERGEANT STONE: You look like a nice well-educated lad. You wouldn't want a reputation as a pornographer, would you?

CHRIS SEALE: You mean like those wank-merchants who peddle degrading images up alleys and give you lot a kick back for turning a blind eye?

But now the copper's getting worked up:

SERGEANT STONE: Right! Enough! Turn this infernal racket down. I can't hear meself think!

Chris complies with this request – the volume is turned down.

CHRIS SEALE: On that, at least, we can agree, Sergeant.

SERGEANT STONE: Let me tell you something, sunbeam: It won't be Virgin Records in court. It won't be Richard Branson. It'll be Regina versus Seale on the charge sheet. One last chance, then next time we come back it'll be <u>you</u> who'll be arrested.

CHRIS SEALE: On what charge? What law has been broken?

Now it's Stone's turn to be flummoxed:

SERGEANT STONE: That remains to be seen. You have been warned.

After they leave Chris's bravado disappears. He mumbles to himself:

CHRIS SEALE: 'I am an anti-christ and I am an anar-chist.' Doesn't even rhyme. Christ!

COMMENTATOR: This is a Call To Adventure…

STORY-TELLER: A what?

COMMENTATOR: Chris has accepted the mantle of Hero. From now on he will be on a Quest for Truth and Justice.

STORY-TELLER: From now on he'll be cacking his velvet loon pants, wondering what he's got himself into and whether it's all worth it… Mind you, the Force must have been in a something of a tiswas themselves when they confabbed with their boss, Inspector Phil Newton.

CUT TO:

INT. INSPECTOR:'S OFFICE. DAY.

Storey and Stone confer with INSPECTOR PHIL NEWTON, *collectively clutching at legal straws to find what law might or might not have been broken:*

INSPECTOR: How about… Corrupting Public Morals?

SERGEANT STONE: It's the best-selling record in the country, Inspector. I'd say the kids are corrupting themselves.

INSPECTOR: Aye. Even our youngster's pogoing around upstairs. I had to buy her a set of headphones so we don't have to endure the racket.

WPC STOREY: There's always… Conspiracy to Cause Public Affray?

INSPECTOR: Um… That <u>has</u> worked against the Unions.

SERGEANT STONE: Last time we went back to King Street the general public weren't tekking a blind bit of notice. We've not had one complaint.

WPC STOREY: That's not exactly the case, Sarge. A Nottingham City Transport Bus Inspector had a word with me after he caught sight of the Virgin Records window out of the top deck. He was most put out.

INSPECTOR: Were there children on the bus?

WPC STOREY: He didn't say… But it must be Obscenity, boss, surely?

INSPECTOR: Legal Definition: A tendency to corrupt or deprave…

SERGEANT STONE: *(not without irony)* With no redeeming social value.

INSPECTOR: Not so easy to secure a conviction on Obscenity since our local filth-monger, D.H. Lawrence, won his case with *Lady Chatterley's Shagger*. And that Virgin wallah Branson's already had his collar felt by the Met's Obscenity Squad… And they drew a blank.

SERGEANT STONE: I hear that lot are as bent as a nine-bob note, guv.

Newton is resolute in his determination to do his duty:

INSPECTOR: Which is an accusation never to be laid at the door of the Notts Constabulary. No! We play this straight. The Chief Constable's taking this personal. You saw him last night on East Midlands Today? He's on a crusade against the morals of today's youth. He reckons they're being led astray by progressive influences, and I reckon he might well be right. The CC is counting on us for a result. Nottingham has to be the test case. Every force in the land is ready to pounce after we secure a guilty verdict. Go back to that shop and arrest the cocky bogger.

SERGEANT STONE: On what charge, guv?

And the Inspector, in his turn, is also flummoxed:

INSPECTOR: You might well ask… *(after a thought)* Pass us down Butterworth Stone's Justice Manual would you, WPC Storey?

WPC STOREY: All three volumes, boss?

The heavy law text books are plonked on the Inspector's desk. He sighs.

INSPECTOR: I'll find something we can get them on… If it takes all night.

CUT TO:

INT. VIRGIN STORE. DAY.

This time it's the Inspector who strides into the store with his Sergeant, and Anarchy In The UK is blasting out.

INSPECTOR: Christopher Searle…

CHRIS SEALE: It's Seale…

INSPECTOR: I am charging you with committing an offence under the terms of the Indecent Advertisement Act…

CHRIS SEALE: The what?

INSPECTOR: Of 1889.

CHRIS SEALE: *(amazed)* 1889?

SERGEANT STONE: Aye. and still on the statute book. Very much so.

INSERT:

A Victorian JUDICIAL VOICE *fades in intoning the terms of this old-fashioned Act:*

JUDICIAL VOICE: Whoever affixes to or inscribes upon any house, building, wall, hoarding, gate, fence, pillar, post, board, tree or on any other place whatsoever so as to be visible to any person being in or passing along any street, public highway or footpath, any picture or printed or written matter which is of an indecent or obscene nature shall, on conviction in manner provided by the jurisdiction of the Act To Suppress Indecent Advertisements, be liable to imprisonment with or without hard labour. Any such advertisement relating to syphilis, gonorrhea, nervous debility, or other complaint or infirmity arising from or relating to sexual intercourse, if it is affixed to or inscribed on any public urinal shall be deemed to be within the meaning of this Act. Any police officer may arrest such a person whom he shall find committing such an offence.

And fades back to the store:

INSPECTOR: You do not have to say anything…

Chris cannot help but mutter under his breath:

CHRIS SEALE: I'll say this is a load of bollocks.

SERGEANT STONE: I heard that!

INSPECTOR: Escort him to Shakespeare Street, Sergeant.

Chris is marched out of the shop.

CUT TO:

INT. POLICE STATION. DAY.

A noisy corridor in the central police station.

STORY-TELLER: So this was the bottom of the barrel that had to be scraped. This was the Law which could be the thin end of a legal wedge to disarm the Pistols. This was an Act drafted to prevent unscrupulous Victorian snake-oil salesmen from purveying shonky cures for VD.

A worried Chris is on the public blower to Branson. It all still seems like a joke to the Virgin boss.

CHRIS SEALE: Richard… I've been arrested.

BRANSON: *(over the phone)* Great! On what charge?

CHRIS SEALE: The Indecent Advertisement Act…

BRANSON: Of 1889!

This knowledge surprises Chris:

CHRIS SEALE: Yeah. You wouldn't believe it.

BRANSON: I would actually, Chris. I've got previous on that… offering medical advice on STDs in my magazine. I got off then and we'll get off now. You know what Oscar Wilde said? 'The only thing worse than being talked about is not being talked about'.

CHRIS SEALE: He might have come to regret that when he was banged up in Reading Gaol. It's not your name on the charge sheet, is it? I could go down for two years.

BRANSON: Bluffing. Six months tops.

CHRIS SEALE: Thanks.

BRANSON: Trust me. I can do Law. My grandfather was a High Court judge. You'll have the finest Defence Lawyer Virgin's money can buy. Keep the faith, brother. After we've won we'll sue the cops for unlawful arrest.

                                                          CUT TO:

INT. VIRGIN OFFICES. DAY.

In Virgin's HQ in 1977 typewriters clatter, old phones ring.

COMMENTATOR: Richard Branson needed a plan. And for this he would need… A Mentor!

STORY-TELLER:	A Lawyer! And by far the most high-profile barrister in the land was Queen's Counsel John Mortimer.
COMMENTATOR:	Later <u>Sir</u> John Mortimer.

Branson is on the phone to louche JOHN MORTIMER: Q.C.

BRANSON:	John…? Richard… Remember the Indecent Advertisements Act…?
MORTIMER:	*(over the phone)* Of 1889?
BRANSON:	They're at it again…

The Cultural Commentator is in her element:

COMMENTATOR:	The Mentor is a mythically sanctioned archetype whose experiential skills must be sought when obstacles stand in the path of the Hero's Quest. Every Oedipus needs a Tiresias. Every Arthur needs a Merlin. Every Bond needs a Q…

But she is shut up:

STORY-TELLER: And every Virgin needs a Rumpole.

The call with Mortimer continues:

BRANSON: They're prosecuting one of my bands – you may have heard of them, The Sex Pistols – for a Word on their album sleeve.

MORTIMER: A Word? What Word?

BRANSON: Bollocks.

MORTIMER: Bollocks? One of my favourite, and indeed, most over-used words.

BRANSON: You'll represent us?

MORTIMER: Naturally. See you back in the Bailey.

BRANSON: Not this time, John… Nottingham Magistrates Court, as it happens.

Now this is a surprise:

MORTIMER: A Q. C. appearing for the Defence before local beaks? They're best served doling out fines for displaying out-of-date tax discs and dogs fouling the pavement.

The usually chortling Branson sounds worried:

BRANSON: I'm rather minded though, if we lose this, they might come after us for a breach of the Obscene Publications Act.

Mortimer is warming to it and offers reassurance:

MORTIMER: Then let me knock them off their provincial perch before it gets that far and save you a fortune, shall we?

BRANSON: Excellent!

MORTIMER: I wouldn't mind a chit chat with your Johnny Rotten. I've seen so many headlines about him since that infamous television appearance.

BRANSON: 'The Filth and the Fury'.

MORTIMER: He sounds like a very interesting young man.

Branson's not so sure:

BRANSON: You're not thinking of calling him, are you?

MORTIMER: I doubt that will be necessary. *(a ponder)* What we need is a lexicographer… An expert in the history of English vernacular.

DISSOLVE TO:

INT. VIRGIN OFFICES. LATER.

Once again Branson is on the phone.

COMMENTATOR: So Branson…

STORY-TELLER: Shameless master of the blower…

COMMENTATOR: Calls up Nottingham University…

STORY-TELLER: Sometimes an alumnus of Stowe can be so persuasive.

Branson's phone manner is indeed beguiling:

BRANSON: Can I speak to your Professor of Linguistics?

He is answered by a brisk university SECRETARY:

SECRETARY: We don't have such a Department… *(after a pause)* I could, however, connect you to the Head of English Studies: Professor Kinsley.

PROF JAMES KINSLEY, *a 'dour' Scot, comes on the line:*

KINSLEY: James Kinsley…

BRANSON: This is Richard Branson, Professor.

The name clearly means nothing and he seems dismissive.

KINSLEY: Is that so?

But Branson persists, mobilising upper-class flattery:

BRANSON: I have it on very good authority that you are the foremost expert on English lexicography.

And Kinsley is indeed flattered:

KINSLEY: That might well be so. My specific area of expertise is the history and development of our native language in the early Middle Ages as evidenced in the minor works of Geoffrey Chaucer.

Can this be the right man for the job?

BRANSON: Oh, really?

KINSLEY: How can I be of help, young man?

Time to lay it on thick:

BRANSON: This is a about a court case of national importance… A matter of artistic freedom… What is in question is the meaning and usage of a Word.

KINSLEY: A Word? What Word?

BRANSON: Bollocks.

Kinsley rolls the Word around his tongue:

KINSLEY: Bollocks? Aye, a most resonant Word with a long-standing pedigree, meanings of which have, rather fascinatedly, transmuted over the centuries. Bollocks! Who is on trial?

BRANSON: A musical combo, actually. Would you be prepared to be an expert witness to defend the use of the Word?

KINSLEY: This is the first time I've been asked. I would be delighted. By the way, would you like me to…

ABRUPT FADE.

The Story-Teller interrupts urgently:

STORY-TELLER: No, wait!!! In the interests of introducing a modicum of Suspense, Professor Kinsley's response must be temporarily withheld.

After this necessary interruption the conversation concludes with Branson reassured and characteristically chuckling again.

BRANSON: That would do nicely, Professor.

DISSOLVE.

HISTORY LESSON.

The Commentator attempts to give her History Lesson – if only she'll be allowed:

COMMENTATOR: Considering the cultural significance of The Sex Pistols from a twenty-first century perspective…

STORY-TELLER: Oh no! Must we?

COMMENTATOR: You said so yourself: Some of us weren't even born.

With some reluctance:

STORY-TELLER: Go on then.

COMMENTATOR: Structurally, this history might be characterised as a binary opposition between two competing Puppet Masters: Manager Malcolm McLaren versus Record Company Owner Richard Branson, for control over four young working-class kids.

STORY-TELLER: It might be… But it might not be true.

COMMENTATOR: The Situationist…

Her attempt to give this lecture will also be continually barracked by the Faginesque tones of MALCOLM McLAREN *declaiming Situationist slogans*:

McLAREN: Be Realistic Demand The Impossible.

COMMENTATOR: …Versus The Capitalist…

And Branson has to make his contribution:

BRANSON: The Sex Pistols could be The Rolling Stones *de nos jours*.

COMMENTATOR: The Art School alumnus…

McLAREN: Take your Desires for Reality.

COMMENTATOR: Versus the Public School Boy.

BRANSON: Signing The Pistols would remove my hippie image at a stroke.

McLAREN: Never trust a Hippie… Especially Mister Pickle.

STORY-TELLER: That was the snarky nickname the Fashionista gave the Businessman in a mistaken belief that Bran<u>son</u> was a scion of the Bran<u>ston</u> Pickle company: 'The iconic kitchen staple since 1923.'

The Commentator persists:

COMMENTATOR: The Provocateur versus The Entrepreneur.

The Story-Teller has had enough:

STORY-TELLER: The Bondage Trousers versus The Woolly Jumper?

McLAREN: Be Everything this Society Hates.

BRANSON: I want that band.

COMMENTATOR: Before they were a Reality this chart-topping pop group was an Idea…

McLAREN: My Idea. *Kutie and the Sex Pistols* made their first appearance as a slogan on one of my over-priced t-shirts from SEX, my King's Road boutique…

COMMENTATOR: Which Malcolm McLaren ran with his partner, Vivienne Westwood.

STORY-TELLER: Later Dame Vivienne Westwood.

COMMENTATOR: Branson's pursuit seemed to be stymied after McLaren signed to EMI for a massive sum.

A cash register rings: kerching! And an upbeat EMI *representative boasts:*

EMI: Thirty thousand pounds!!!

McLAREN: Cash For Chaos.

COMMENTATOR: Before the label almost immediately dropped the controversial band with a massive pay-off.

The cash register rings again, but now the voice is far from upbeat:

EMI: Twenty thousand pounds!!!

BRANSON: Now I was certain my persistence to sign the band would finally be rewarded. I went round to EMI to meet their manager and cement the deal.

COMMENTATOR: This was the first time the two Svengalis would make eye contact.

CUT AWAY TO:

INSERT. INT. EMI HQ. DAY.

Bonhomie apparently prevails:

McLAREN: Richard! I'll bring the boys round to you at Virgin this afternoon.

BRANSON: Malcolm! Excellent. A done deal at last.

But for how long?

BRANSON: But they never showed up. And I was to read in the music press that McLaren had signed The Pistols to A&M Records for an even more outrageous sum.

The cash register rings again and now it's an upbeat A&M executive who crows:

A&M: Fifty thousand pounds!

BRANSON: Foiled again!

STORY-TELLER: Much to the disgust of A&M's co-founder Herb Alpert of Tijuana Brass fame, trumpeting auteur of *Spanish Flea*.

COMMENTATOR: Not without good reason…

INSERT:

INT. A & M RECORDS OFFICE. DAY.

A very raucous party. Beer cans opening. Smashing glasses, squirmy sex, violent puking.

COMMENTATOR: At a celebratory party following the infamous photo-op of The Sex Pistols signing the contract outside Buckingham Palace the band wrecks the offices of their current record company, where their new bassist, Sid Vicious...

STORY-TELLER: Never been known to play a note...

COMMENTATOR: Allegedly vomited over the desk of A&M's MD.

A last gasp?

McLAREN: Be Childish. Be Irresponsible. Be Disrespectful.

COMMENTATOR: They were dropped less than a week later...

35

STORY-TELLER: With an even greater pay-off.

The cash register rings and now it's the A&M exec who is downbeat:

A&M: Twenty-five thousand pounds!

END OF INSERT.

McLAREN: Rot and Roll! My orchestrated smash-and-grab raids on the capitalist record industry earned The Sex Pistols the accolade of 'Young Businessmen of the Year' from *Investors Review*.

BRANSON: Now Virgin was the only game in town. At last I would be able to get hold of the band… *(sniggering)* For an undisclosed sum. A cut-price deal.

The cash register rings for the last time.

McLAREN: A terrible calamity. The worst mistake The Sex Pistols ever made.

Branson chortles characteristically:

BRANSON: From the moment I signed the band McLaren was looking for ways to alienate us so we'd be sufficiently embarrassed and want to get rid of them. To his horror I refused to be outraged. So it was Virgin Records which released the single, *God Save The Queen*, to coincide with the Silver Jubilee in June.

COMMENTATOR: Despite being banned by the BBC it sold one hundred thousand copies.

STORY-TELLER: As I recall the 'official' Top Of The Pops was, appropriately enough, Rod Stewart's *I Don't Want To Talk About It*.

COMMENTATOR: Virgin rush-released the album. Facing manufactured media outrage and High Street bans, advance orders of more than one hundred and fifty thousand were enough to send *Never Mind The Bollocks Here's The Sex Pistols* soaring into the charts at Number One!

Branson is triumphant:

BRANSON: No-one could ever again accuse me of being a boring young fart presiding over an unhip prog-rock label.

And McLaren far from so:

McLAREN: The Society Of The Spectacle Is All Around.

COMMENTATOR: It was Branson, not McLaren, who had taken on the role of the Trickster.

STORY-TELLER: The what-ster?

She has her chance – thanks for asking!

COMMENTATOR: The Trickster is a mythical archetype. Existing in the Liminal Zone where normal rules no longer apply, the Trickster's imperative is to destabilise. *Agent provocateur,* Lord of Misrule… The Trickster enjoys his work. Every day is Saturnalia.

STORY-TELLER: Fair enough, I suppose. This story has no shortage of Tricksters. McLaren; Branson, Rotten…

Her last chance – for now.

COMMENTATOR: Even John Mortimer Q.C. – who'd have a few tricks up his sleeve before that train trip from Saint Pancras up to the East Midlands for an appearance before the provincial tribunal.

STORY-TELLER: Oh, to have been a fly on the wall on that one and only meeting in the legal chambers of the Mutual Admiration Society of two Johns: Uncle Mortimer and Bad Lad Lydon.

CUT TO:

INT. MORTIMER'S CHAMBERS. DAY.

JOHN LYDON *and John Mortimer meet. The former is at first, naturally, somewhat sneery and wary whilst the latter is, of course, entirely at home, suave and avuncular.*

LYDON: Well, Mister Queen's Counsel…

MORTIMER: Well, Mister Rotten…

LYDON: My name's John.

MORTIMER: So is mine.

LYDON: Another one of the Johns, eh? Brilliant.

MORTIMER: Your reputation precedes you, John.

LYDON: Don't believe everything you read in the papers, John.

MORTIMER: Yes, it would be terrible to think that a democracy is run by tabloid newspapers… Or, indeed, in your case, teatime television.

LYDON: So we swore on the Today show. Big fucking deal.

MORTIMER: And I quote: ' "I Kicked In My TV Set" says Angry Father of Four!'

LYDON: Perfect British comedy.

MORTIMER: I always wanted to be a star of musical comedy.

	But as I can't sing, dance or play the piano that was a pretty hopeless aspiration. Your performance, however, has made Johnny Rotten something of a national hate-figure.
LYDON:	That creepshow sleaze-bag arsehole Bill Grundy was even more shit-faced than we were.
MORTIMER:	I've always found alcohol to be entirely conducive for oiling the wheels of the creative process. When I'm working on a play I get up about six o'clock in the morning, like a farmer, and scribble until lunchtime. Then I get drunk… *(after a pause)* Not <u>too</u> drunk.
LYDON:	You have something of a reputation yourself. They call you a Champagne Socialist.
MORTIMER:	You <u>can</u> believe some things you read in the press. Marx (Karl of that ilk, not Groucho) may have said (and if he didn't he should have) that under socialism the proletariat would be travelling first class and drinking shampers… Talking of bubbles, it's after lunchtime… almost. Would you care to join me in a glass of the widow?
LYDON:	The what?
MORTIMER:	The blessèd Oscar's name for Veuve Cliquot.
LYDON:	Oh, Mister Wilde. Beardie Branson's source of what passes for wit. I'd prefer a more proletarian tipple.
MORTIMER:	I'm sure that can be arranged.

A champagne cork is popped and a beer can ring-pull is opened. Drinks are poured and supped.

MORTIMER:	Your manager, I understand, is inspired by more Gallic influences?

LYDON: *(sneering)* Situationism?

MORTIMER: Soixante-huit and all that.

LYDON: Soixante-fucking-neuf in that cunt's case. Paris sixty-eight was ten years ago. There's a common misconception that Malcolm McLaren pulls my strings for some art school student provocation foolishness. That's just not true. I'm nobody's puppet.

MORTIMER: That I can believe. *(after a pause)* I must say, those are a rather curious pair of trousers. Zips up the back? I have enough trouble remembering to do up the one at the front. Why all those safety pins?

LYDON: Why the wig and gown?

MORTIMER: Necessary garb of the Theatre of the Law, I'm afraid. Your's, I presume, is the mandatory uniform of Punk?

LYDON: I've come to detest that word. I refuse to allow it to be applied to me.

MORTIMER: In the American prison system 'punk', I'm informed, refers to a 'catamite'.

LYDON: See what I mean?

MORTIMER: Besides I won't need to get dragged up for an appearance before the Nottingham bench. A sober suit suffices.

LYDON: Have you heard our record, John?

MORTIMER: Would that really be necessary, John?

LYDON: Have you seen us play?

MORTIMER: How could I? It would seem you've been censored by every Watch Committee and Local Council in the land.

LYDON: Fine with me. We must be doing something right. Who knows? The Pistols might turn you on. My performance was modelled on Olivier as Richard the Third.

MORTIMER: Splendid! I'll pass on that accolade to Larry when next we drink champagne together at the National. I've no doubt he'll be honoured by the compliment. *(after a pause)* Now about this case...

They're enjoying the drinks... and each other's company.

LYDON: Malcolm wants nothing to do with it. He thinks it's some posh-boy wheeze. He wants us to lose.

MORTIMER: I've not been engaged by Malcolm McLaren but by Richard Branson.

LYDON: I rather like 'Call-Me-Richard'. A public school boy to the nth degree.

MORTIMER: As indeed am I.

LYDON: With him everything is a game. He sees this trial as jolly good fun.

MORTIMER: But he's very serious about winning. What about you, John? Do you want us to win or lose?

LYDON: The Sex Pistols aren't self-destructive – quite the opposite. We might be out to wreck the system... certainly not to wreck ourselves.

MORTIMER: I do hope that's true... *(a pause)* To prepare my case I'd better know how you came up with the Word.

LYDON: What's the point trying to take credit for that title? Malcolm wanted: *God Save The Sex Pistols,* would you believe? I don't believe in God and I don't need saving… except perhaps from our manager. I certainly didn't relish sitting around while he wanked on with his Situationist so-called philosophy. Yawn.

It was Steve Jones, our kleptomaniac guitarist, who came out with: *Never Mind The Bollocks* – a hackneyed catch-phrase he picked up from two hard-case brothers of his dubious acquaintance who preside over a hot-dog stand in Piccadilly.

There was no great master plan. No genius. A really horrible, cheesy cover with absolutely no consideration about artistic merit. Vomit yellow and puke pink. Now, of course, it's become the punk Venus de Milo and everyone is taking credit.

MORTIMER: I was rather taken with the cut-out words.

LYDON: That concept comes from a blackmail letter.

MORTIMER: One of our fellow wordsmiths, whose name now eludes me, once declared that the only writing which ever made any money was a ransom note.

They are getting increasingly pissed and increasingly bonding.

LYDON: Brilliant. We held them to ransom and they paid up. *(with passion)* Who has the right to tell me what words I can or cannot use? Unacceptable! We are humans who created this wonderful thing called language. This is what we're supposed to do as a species: Advance ideas. Rebellious youth culture is absolutely essential. Words are my weapons. This is not some fashion statement!

MORTIMER: Bravo! But you do realise that, should we lose, they'll quite possibly be coming after you?

LYDON: What do you think has been going on these past two years? I want you in my corner, Mister Mortimer. You won't put up with supporting a lemon.

MORTIMER: I'll demolish this ridiculous prosecution. That's what I'm paid to do. But I'm not going to risk calling you as a Witness for the Defence. I would, however, expect you to be there to watch the system in action. See you in court, John... in the Public Gallery.

CUT TO:

INT. HOTEL ROOM. NIGHT.

Throbbing Dub Reggae and Australian bush ballads!

STORY-TELLER: On the Eve of Battle Lydon came up to our town, Nottingham, to give 'moral support' and for the optics in court the following morning, holing up with a motley coterie under a pseudonymous alias, at the quasi-posh Albany Hotel on Maid Marian Way...

COMMENTATOR: Probably the ugliest road in Europe.

At this he must concur.

STORY-TELLER: Wouldn't have been much fun for any travelling business-person attempting a good night's sleep in an adjoining room as Dub Reggae from U Roy *et al* from Jamaica sequed into, perhaps surprisingly, raucous stomps by The Bushwackers Band from Down Under. But the agèd Night Porter, repeatedly summoned to replenish ever diminishing stocks of cans of Carlsberg...

COMMENTATOR: Probably the best lager in the world?

At this he has to snort.

STORY-TELLER: … Found the pie-eyed occupant of room Seven Hundred and Fifteen to be extremely polite. The penny finally dropped: This young lad was tabloid Public Enemy Number One!

The NIGHT PORTER *is a jovial Nottingham chap in his 60s. A revelation:*

NIGHT PORTER: Ere! You're 'im!

LYDON: *(slurring)* So it would seem.

NIGHT PORTER: Would you give us an autograph, me duck? Not for mesen, you know. Me grand-daughter's a great fan o' yourn.

LYDON: With great pleasure, dear sir. How old is she?

NIGHT PORTER: Fourteen.

LYDON: Ah! The future!

He willingly signs a crumpled napkin.

NIGHT PORTER: You're such a nice lad. You wouldn't think you was Johnny Rotten, would you?

COMMENTATOR: The party would go on until four-thirty a.m.

CUT TO:

EXT. HOTEL LOBBY. MORNING.

Lydon slumps out of the hotel.

STORY-TELLER: A few short hours later, in the early morning light, a doubtless groggy John Lydon dons tartan bondage trousers and, from the voluminous collection of his headgear, he chooses to adopt for the occasion… the iconic titfer of the British Raj: A solar topee!

COMMENTATOR: Emerging from the hotel lobby, Johnny is met by a young policeman.

Outside the hotel a young CONSTABLE *approaches Lydon:*

CONSTABLE: My orders are to escort you to the Guildhall, Mister Rotten.

Unsurprisingly greeted with some degree of sarcasm:

LYDON: Why? Do you think I might get lost on the way, Mister Plod?

CONSTABLE: It's for your own safety… Mind you, I reckon that's perfectly possible. *(as they walk).* Would you mind signing my copy of *Anarchy*? I bought it at Virgin Records on King Street. A first pressing. Might be worth something some day.

This entreaty is not treated with such good grace:

STORY-TELLER: Best to blur Johnny's far from courteous expletive ridden response to <u>this</u> request for an autograph.

Bleep bleep bleep!

CUT TO:

INT. NOTTINGHAM MAGISTRATES COURT. DAY.

The hubbub of the provincial court.

COMMENTATOR: Nottingham Magistrates Court, Thursday, November the Twenty-Fourth, 1977. Regina versus Seale.

STORY-TELLER: Mortimer is out on parade that chill November morning with Chris Seale in the dock and Richard Branson in the packed Public Gallery to watch his employee plead:

CHRIS SEALE: Not Guilty.

COMMENTATOR: By the time John Lydon eventually fronts up the trial has already commenced. Other members of the band were expected to turn out in force...

STORY-TELLER: Needless to say, they missed the train – should they have ever attempted to catch it – and never bothered to show. Perhaps for the best.

COMMENTATOR: Three volunteer Magistrates, two of them women whose identities remain shrouded in mystery, will preside and determine the record store worker's fate, under the chairmanship of sexagenarian...

DOUGLAS BETTS *sounds so proud... for now:*

BETTS: Douglas Betts... Magistrate.

COMMENTATOR: Surely those local worthies on the Bench, appointed protectors of public morality called upon to maintain social control through artistic repression, must have been anxious that they'd be out of their depth when faced by such an eminent Queen's Counsel. Surely they must have been apprehensive to learn that the Prosecution responded to this provocation by also securing the services of yet another Queens Counsel.

STORY-TELLER: Surely David Ritchie Q.C. could be no relation to that barely competent bassist Simon John Ritchie a.k.a. Sid Vicious?

COMMENTATOR: Surely Prosecutor Ritchie might have considered such a high-profile trial would be his moment in the spotlight…

STORY-TELLER: A chance for fame and glory.

COMMENTATOR: Surely he thought he would go down in history as the sledgehammer to crack these nuts, to break this butterfly upon a wheel.

STORY-TELLER: Should have been a cut-and-dried formality.

COMMENTATOR: But today would be the Prosecution's performance on trial.

STORY-TELLER: This was never going to be a normal day in Nottingham Guildhall.

COMMENTATOR: David Ritchie Q.C. opens for the Crown.

DAVID RITCHIE Q.C.? *Who knows? An upper-crust London lawyer? He rises to give his opening address:*

RITCHIE: There are those who might assert that the Indecent Advertisement Act of 1889 is an antediluvian piece of legislation. Let me assure you it is anything but.

The Act is alive and kicking and as applicable now as when it was first drafted for the protection of the populace. It is certainly not a dead letter, every bit as relevant to our life in the twentieth century. Should guilt be proven this morning, as I have no doubt it must, this flagrant flaunting of the law of the land might well, I'm sure Your Worships would concur, provoke a more serious charge to take place in a higher court before a jury of reasonable men and women who would surely consider this an outrageous obscenity, as any right-thinking citizen must do.

Mortimer whispers to his client:

MORTIMER: So that _is_ what they're after!

RITCHIE: The defendant, Christopher Seale, Manager of the Virgin Record store in the very centre of this city, was requested to remove the odious album cover from open display no less than four times before his eventual arrest. After the first polite warning, not only was this simple injunction blatantly disobeyed but a huge poster of the record cover, measuring nine feet by six feet, was prominently exhibited and which is now displayed in court before you. The Word stood out, blatantly contravening any standard of decency under the terms of this Act.

STORY-TELLER: Exhibit A.

Ritchie continues:

RITCHIE: It is not, however, the disgusting B-word alone which should be construed as being obscene by itself. It was the cumulative effect of the material as a whole and the juxtaposition of the offending Word with 'The Sex Pistols' which would knowingly be guaranteed to cause indecency.

Again Mortimer whispers to his client:

MORTIMER: All is revealed, Chris. It's not _you_ but The Sex Pistols who are on trial.

COMMENTATOR: Ritchie calls his first and only witness for the Crown: arresting officer, Sergeant Raymond George Stone.

STORY-TELLER: Taking the stand, the Sarge plods through the procedure of the arrest on oath and for the record... No need to put this formality out on parade.

COMMENTATOR: Ritchie's one and only question to the policeman:

RITCHIE: Sergeant Stone, why did the Nottinghamshire Constabulary engage upon this action?

Mortimer stands to object:

MORTIMER: Speculation! How is a humble uniformed Sergeant of the Nottinghamshire Constabulary expected to be cognisant of the machinations of his Chief Constable?

The Prosecutor is spluttering:

RITCHIE: That is a most outrageous suggestion, Your Worships…

Betts sighs:

BETTS: Let him answer!

Which he does with some reluctance:

SERGEANT STONE: We did this to prevent millions of people having such filth inflicted upon them.

In the Public Gallery Richard Branson can't help but laugh out loud:

BRANSON: Millions? If only!

The Court USHER has to intervene:

USHER: Silence!

COMMENTATOR: Mortimer rises to cross-examine. He passes over a copy of a daily paper to the witness box…

STORY-TELLER: Which seems to come as a surprise to the copper.

MORTIMER: Sergeant Stone, could you identify this for the court?

49

SERGEANT STONE: Well... It's a newspaper.

MORTIMER: The Guardian, in fact.

STORY-TELLER: Exhibit B.

Punk record is a load of legal trouble

MORTIMER: Of what date?

SERGEANT STONE: November the Tenth.

MORTIMER: Remind the court... on what date was my client arrested?

SERGEANT STONE: November the Ninth.

MORTIMER: This national paper was therefore published on the day following the arrest of Mister Seale under the terms of the Indecent Advertisement Act of 1889?

SERGEANT STONE: So it would seem.

MORTIMER: Could you turn to page five and read the headline.

If he must – pages are turned and he reads:

SERGEANT STONE: 'Punk Record Is A Load of Legal Trouble.'

MORTIMER: Legal trouble precipitated, no doubt, by you and your colleagues! Could you tell Their Worships what picture accompanies that article?

Like pulling teeth:

SERGEANT STONE: A record cover.

MORTIMER: Indeed. The title of which is? In full if you please, Sergeant Stone.

Spitting it out:

SERGEANT STONE: 'Never Mind The Bollocks Here's the Sex Pistols.'

Mortimer is clearly getting what he wants:

MORTIMER: Is not that the very record sleeve for which you arrested the defendant for displaying? Reproduced in full, entire and unexpurgated?

SERGEANT STONE: So it would seem.

MORTIMER: Then I ask you, Sergeant Stone, why officers of the Nottinghamshire Constabulary were not also instructed to arrest newsagents who were selling such a widely available newspaper?

Chairman Douglas Betts makes another weary interjection:

BETTS: Newsagents! What have they got to do with it?

MORTIMER: I am merely trying, Your Worship, to establish the motives behind the police prosecution – or should I say persecution – of an employee of a record shop.

At this Ritchie must splutter:

RITCHIE: An astonishing suggestion!

MORTIMER: No further questions.

Mortimer sits and Ritchie rises. Could it be that the Prosecutor is already aware he is losing this game?

RITCHIE: The case for the Prosecution rests.

Ritchie slumps down.

COMMENTATOR: Mortimer's first witness for the Defence would be Caroline Coon, a talented artist and fearless activist as the founder of Release…

STORY-TELLER: First port of call for young people and pop star victims fitted up or busted in the so-called 'War Against Drugs'.

COMMENTATOR: John Mortimer had called her for the Defence in the Oz trial of 1971 when the publishers of the notorious underground magazine…

STORY-TELLER: Which you never bought…

COMMENTATOR: … stood trial on serious charges of Obscenity and Conspiracy: 'To debauch and corrupt the morals of young children'.

STORY-TELLER: I still have my copy… probably worth a few quid now.

COMMENTATOR: Mortimer lost that case…

STORY-TELLER: But the verdict was over-turned on appeal. Caroline Coon was no stranger to law courts and had no fear of coppers in uniform or old men in wigs.

COMMENTATOR: Perhaps the main reason Mortimer wanted her on the stand was that she was one of the first and most articulate chroniclers in the music press to recognise the historical importance of this cultural phenomenon.

STORY-TELLER: Is that what it was? Wished I'd've known when I was pogo-ing and getting gobbed on.

COMMENTATOR: If anyone was qualified to testify for the significance of The Sex Pistols it was Caroline Coon.

Mortimer stands to question CAROLINE COON:. *Her voice may sound 'posh', but her attitudes are 'street-smart'.*

MORTIMER: Ms Coon, how would you describe this so-called movement of Punk Rock?

CAROLINE COON: It's a wonderful protest of disenfranchised youth who feel this country offers them no future. Nothing like it has been seen in England for the last ten years.

MORTIMER: Do you consider Punk Rock to be a threat to society?

Again Betts interjects, ever more fatigued:

BETTS: Really, what has this to do with the simple charge before us?

Mortimer is always ultimately polite:

MORTIMER: Would Your Worships please allow my witness to answer the question?

BETTS: *(sighing)* Get on with it!

CAROLINE COON: Certainly it might be seen as a threat… But only to those aspects of society which need to be challenged.

MORTIMER: What, then, do you think is the meaning of the title of the record?

CAROLINE COON: Well, there has been so much sensationalist misinformation written about The Sex Pistols and their followers in the national press. The title obviously means: 'Forget all the lies and listen to the music.'

Ritchie snorts loudly:

RITCHIE: Music!

MORTIMER: As a prominent cultural commentator, Ms Coon, what do you consider to be the validity of *Never Mind The Bollocks Here's The Sex Pistols*?

CAROLINE COON: The album is in the best rebellious tradition of rock and roll. But it speaks in the language of the world we live in today. That, for me, is the measure of great art.

Another obvious snort from the Prosecution:

RITCHIE: Art!

MORTIMER: Then why, in your opinion, has this prosecution been brought?

CAROLINE COON: This would seem to be yet another attempt by the Powers That Be to suppress freedom of expression.

MORTIMER: Thank you, Ms Coon.

Mortimer sits and Ritchie rises for the cross-examination:

RITCHIE: Are you aware, <u>Miss</u> Coon, that in one song on this LP record a word was used even more disgusting than the Word on the cover?

CAROLINE COON: Which word is that?

RITCHIE: I do not have to say what it was. Is there such a song?

CAROLINE COON: What song?

RITCHIE: Is there such a word?

CAROLINE COON: What word?

RITCHIE: I am asking you, Miss Coon, whether the word 'fuck' is in a song on the album?

This seems to surprise her:

CAROLINE COON: Is it? I don't think so.

RITCHIE: Are you certain of that?

CAROLINE COON: Before I could give an absolute answer, I would need to listen to the album.

RITCHIE: Surely, you <u>have</u> listened to the 'album'? You have, I believe, given it a 'rave review'. You would, therefore, know whether the word 'fuck' appears in a song or not.

CAROLINE COON: It's not always easy to make out some of the words. Unless I had a copy of the lyrics I could not give an answer with certainty.

RITCHIE: But as far as you recollect?

CAROLINE COON: The word may or may not appear.

RITCHIE: I put it to you that the album has only sold in such large numbers because of its use of salacious material.

CAROLINE COON: Not at all. It's because of the music.

RITCHIE: Some might call it so. Would you continue to defend the album if the word 'fuck' <u>was</u> in the title?

CAROLINE COON: But it isn't, is it? No record company in their right mind would be prepared to do that, realising full well the likely consequences.

RITCHIE: So 'bollocks' is acceptable but 'fuck' is not?

CAROLINE COON: You haven't said where that word does appear.

RITCHIE: Are you familiar with the word 'fuck', Miss Coon?

She can barely suppress her scorn:

CAROLINE COON: I would like to think I know what that word means. I'm a grown woman. I'm over thirty.

RITCHIE: I find that hard to believe… *(a pause)* I mean that you are over thirty.

COMMENTATOR: Another misogynistic sleaze bag.

RITCHIE: No further questions.

COMMENTATOR: Increasingly evident that it was not a Word on trial but the popularity and influence of The Sex Pistols. The Prosecution was already on the back foot when Mortimer called his final…

STORY-TELLER: … and most devastating…

COMMENTATOR: … Expert Witness for the Defence: James Kinsley.

Professor James Kinsley takes the stand.

MORTIMER: Could you tell this court why you have been called here today, Professor Kinsley?

KINSLEY: I am Head of English Studies at the University of Nottingham.

MORTIMER: And you are, I believe, an authority in…?

KINSLEY: Medieval English Linguistics.

Ritchie rises to make a limp objection:

RITCHIE: I fail to see what possible relevance the testimony of this witness, whatever his academic credentials, could have to contribute to the case before us.

MORTIMER: This is precisely what the Defence wishes to establish.

The Chairman is increasingly frustrated:

BETTS: I'm a bit perplexed myself. But we'll indulge you, Mister Mortimer… I suppose.

The Story-Teller butts in to provide some context:

STORY-TELLER: According to a good friend of mine, employed to serve as a young foot-soldier in the university department dominated by this towering presence, Professor Kinsley had a fondness for neither students nor literary studies…

COMMENTATOR: Minimum requirements, it might be thought, for such a post. Making him something of a joke to more progressive lecturers in his department…

STORY-TELLER: For Kinsley, big bad Virginia Woolf would be nothing to be afraid of. T. S. Eliot would be an anagram for 'toilets'. And he apparently refused even to set foot in Eastwood, the 'country of the heart' for local hero D.H. Lawrence.

COMMENTATOR: Paradoxically, however, wilful ignorance of twentieth century modernist literature would make Professor Kinsley the ideal expert witness for the Defence… Because he had one other qualification which made his presence in the courtroom ungainsayable…

She is cut off abruptly:

STORY-TELLER: No, stop!!! This tantalisingly revelation must continue to be a mystery withheld…

In the Magistrates Court Mortimer begins the examination of his crucial witness:

MORTIMER: Professor Kinsley, you have come here today willingly…

KINSLEY: And without payment…

MORTIMER: … to testify that the basis of the Prosecution's attempt to suppress a Word on the sleeve of a pop music long playing record is unfounded?

KINSLEY: That is so.

MORTIMER: And indeed malicious?

KINSLEY: That must, perforce, also be so.

MORTIMER: The Word in question…

KINSLEY: Bollocks!

MORTIMER: Yes. This is an ancient term in our language, is it not?

KINSLEY: Indeed it is. The Word has been found in written records dating back before the year one thousand anno domini.

MORTIMER: Predating the Norman Conquest! What <u>then</u> was the meaning of the Word?

KINSLEY: The Word originally meant 'a small ball' and subsequently came to be used for other such objects of an appropriate shape. Thus it came to be applied to orchids.

Mortimer purports to be surprised:

MORTIMER: Orchids, Professor?

KINSLEY: Presumably on account of the organic resemblance of an aspect of those flowers. Obviously to the shape of male genitalia.

MORTIMER: Ah, I see! There are, I believe, literary references?

KINSLEY: Most certainly. The Word is used in the Bible.

At this Ritchie is ball-istic:

RITCHIE: Not in my Bible!

KINSLEY: Then I assume you may not be conversant with Wycliffe's first English vernacular version from Thirteen Eighty Two where he renders Leviticus Chapter Twenty-Two, Verse Twenty-Four as: *(adopting a scholarly tone)* 'Al beeste ye shulen not offre to the Lord that are kilt and taken awey the ballokes.'

MORTIMER: Could you please translate this fourteenth century text for Their Worships?

KINSLEY: A perfectly clear instance of the medieval usage of the Word for 'testicles'. The King James Authorised Version renders this, perhaps more euphemistically, as: 'Ye shall not offer unto the Lord that which is bruised or crushed or broken or cut.'

MORTIMER: Meaning?

KINSLEY: A Biblical injunction that no animals should be offered for sacrifice which have been castrated… That is to say that their bollocks have been cut off.

MORTIMER: The Word, I am told, also appears in place names?

KINSLEY: Certainly. There is, in the New Forest, a Sandy Ballocks.

MORTIMER: Presumably without proving undue difficulty for local residents… Much as for those who now live in Maidenhead?

Laughter. Lydon guffaws in the Public Gallery.

BETTS: Mister Mortimer, this is not Sunday Night at the London Palladium. Get on with it!

MORTIMER: *(to the Bench)* Would that I could, Your Worships. But I'm afraid there are several etymological centuries still remaining. *(to Kinsley)* Any other meanings, Professor Kinsley, in the long history of the Word which might possibly be deemed offensive?

KINSLEY: Offensive? I think not.

MORTIMER: But in popular parlance?

KINSLEY: By obvious extension, towards the end of the eighteenth century 'bollocks' came to mean: 'balls'.

MORTIMER: In the sense of…?

KINSLEY: 'Rubbish'.

MORTIMER: Ah, I see! What, then, do you think is the meaning of the title of this pop music record?

KINSLEY: I would take the cover of the album, as has been shown to me, to import: 'Never Mind The Nonsense – Listen to the Sex Pistols.'

MORTIMER: Could there perhaps be any further meaning of which the magistrates should be appraised, Professor?

KINSLEY: Well… in an authoritative nineteenth-century Dictionary of Slang there is an intriguing reference from the 1860s which cites the Officer Commanding the Straits Fleet referring to his Chaplain as 'Bollocks the Rector', clearly evidencing that the Word had become a nickname for clergymen.

Mortimer feigns amazement:

MORTIMER: Clergymen! Why would that that be?

KINSLEY: Aye, well, during their sermons, men of the cloth are well known to talk nonsense.

MORTIMER: You speak with some authority in this regard, do you not, Professor Kinsley?

KINSLEY: I do indeed.

MORTIMER: If it please the court, would you roll down the neck of your sweater?

KINSLEY: Most certainly.

Past the point of no return:

BETTS: Is this really necessary?

Kinsley's turtle-neck is theatrically rolled down.

KINSLEY: You see that I wear a dog collar.

MORTIMER: So as well being an expert lexicographer in the history and development of the English language you are also a clergyman?

KINSLEY: I am an ordained priest of the Anglican Church and can personally vouch for the accuracy that clergy are known to spout a great deal of bollocks.

The people in the Public Gallery applaud. Lydon whoops.

STORY-TELLER: Now it can be revealed: The hitherto concealed query Professor Kinsley had put to Branson on that phone call when he first agreed to testify.

CUT AWAY TO:

FLASHBACK. PHONE CALL WITH BRANSON. FROM BEFORE:

KINSLEY: By the way, would you like me to wear my dog collar in court?

BRANSON: That would do nicely, Professor.

CUT BACK TO:

INT. NOTTINGHAM MAGISTRATE'S COURT. AS BEFORE.

STORY-TELLER: Thought it was worth waiting for. Now the Crown is really bollocksed.

Back in court Ritchie is increasingly floundering:

COMMENTATOR: Ritchie rises to cross-examine Professor Kinsley.

RITCHIE: You claim to be a 'linguistic expert', Professor Kinsley, and you have spoken with apparent authority on the derivation of the controversial Word…

And Kinsley is enjoying it:

KINSLEY: Bollocks. Controversial? I think not.

RITCHIE: But I ask you, what about 'fuck', 'shit', 'cunt'? Would you be prepared to defend the use of these words? Are these words in the Oxford English Dictionary?

KINSLEY: The Shorter or the Longer? I have not been asked to bring a copy of either with me. I am certain, though, that if they are not, they should be.

Chairman Betts is at his wit's end:

BETTS: Enough!

And Ritchie realises he is defeated:

RITCHIE: No further questions.

COMMENTATOR: Mortimer surely earned his fee that morning when he rose to make his closing speech.

Mortimer stands:

MORTIMER: The use of the English language should not be a criminal matter, Your Worships. What sort of country are we living in if, say, a politician comes to Nottingham and speaks to a group of people in the city centre and during his speech a heckler shouts: 'Bollocks'? Are we to expect this person to be arrested and incarcerated?

Or do we live in a country where we are proud of our vernacular? Do we wish our language to be virile and strong or watered down and weak? Do we want blanks, asterisks or bleeps which people can easily fill in with their own imagination? Or are we strong enough to tolerate, indeed to support, our vivid Anglo-Saxon language even if some puritanical minds don't approve? If a Word is on the lips of the people, why should it not be on the cover of a long-playing record? 'Bollocks' may be impolite or vulgar, but to say something is 'a load of bollocks' should that incur a criminal prosecution? While 'bollocks' might well be immodest it would require a giant leap for the Word to be considered 'indecent'.

Ritchie makes one last limp objection:

RITCHIE: There can be no such separation. Immodest is indecent. Under the terms of the Act 'bollocks' is indecent.

Mortimer ignores this.

BETTS: Carry on, Mister Mortimer… If you must.

MORTIMER: Why should a Word which has been dignified in our native tongue from before the Middle Ages be singled out for prosecution because it is on a record sleeve? I wonder, as I'm sure you must do, Your Worships, what the world is to think about a judicial system in this country, this city, which has to squander its time in consideration of a Word used to describe a load of balderdash?

The truth is that it was the lurid visage of the album itself that has been on trial for Indecency. Because what really offends the authorities is not the Word but the very existence of The Sex Pistols and the young people who follow them. This case doesn't just raise the question of freedom of speech and the censorship of artistic expression, but the sinister suggestion of a possible police conspiracy.

For the Prosecutor such a suggestion must be outrageous:

RITCHIE:　　　　　I object!

BETTS:　　　　　*(fed up with it)* Mister Ritchie, this is Nottingham Magistrates Court not an episode of Perry Mason.

MORTIMER:　　　It is because of The Sex Pistols that this prosecution was brought and not the music of Donald Duck or Kathleen Ferrier…

A startled Story-Teller feels he has to interrupt:

STORY-TELLER:　Hang on a minute, John Mortimer Q.C.! Donald Duck? Not best known as a recording artiste. What's this about? John Lydon's cartoonish vocal prowess?

COMMENTATOR:　The choice of Kathleen Ferrier was perhaps a more pertinent reference to the musical taste of those provincial Magistrates.

The beloved contralto sings, to the tune of 'The Keel Row':

KATHLEEN FERRIER:　As I walked doon King Street
　　　　　　　　　　Doon King Street, doon King Street
　　　　　　　　　　As I walked doon King Street
　　　　　　　　　　I heard a lassie say:
　　　　　　　　　　Never Mind the Bollocks,
　　　　　　　　　　the Bollocks, the Bollocks
　　　　　　　　　　Never Mind the Bollocks
　　　　　　　　　　Here's The Sex Pistols.

STORY-TELLER:　What is life?

Mortimer concludes:

MORTIMER: I have nothing further to add, Your Worships. 'Put aside all other rubbish and pay attention to what's on the record'. That is the meaning of the title.

COMMENTATOR: The Magistrates withdraw.

A match is struck.

STORY-TELLER: Sitting in the Public Gallery, Johnny Rotten lights up a fag…

The Usher barks out:

USHER: Put that cigarette out or leave this court!

COMMENTATOR: After only twenty minutes deliberation, Douglas Betts and the other two magistrates return to the Bench.

BETTS: Christopher Seale, you will stand. *(he does)*
After due deliberation, much as my colleagues and I wholeheartedly deplore the vulgar exploitation of the worst instincts of human nature for the purpose of commercial profit, we must <u>reluctantly</u> find you Not Guilty.

COMMENTATOR: Case dismissed.

Chris breathes a sigh of relief as he is applauded from the Gallery.

STORY-TELLER: They fought the Law… and the Law lost!
<u>Reluctantly.</u>

CUT TO:

EXT. MAGISTRATES COURT. DAY.

Outside the court:

COMMENTATOR: The relieved defendant, Chris Seale, is photographed posing with the album which might well have brought his reputation into disrepute…

A celebratory Branson pops a champagne cork.

STORY-TELLER: Only to be side-lined as a beaming Branson pops a celebratory cork.

BRANSON: What a result! Never doubted it for a moment.

>   Get our poster out of that court room, Chris, and
>   back in Virgin's window. I predict a busy
>   afternoon.

A triumphant Lydon joins the throng:

LYDON: Bollocks is legal! Bollocks! Bollocks! Bollocks!

COMMENTATOR: Before he left town Johnny Rotten guested on a local radio station…

CUT TO:

INT. LOCAL RADIO STATION. DAY.

Lydon is interviewed:

LYDON: We fought them in court and we won! Heaven forbid if politicians or Mary Whitehouse or whoever liked anything we did… that would be slash-your-wrists time for me. If you believe in what you are doing then nothing can stop you. I'd like to dedicate this Cliff Richard song to Mister No-Show Malcolm McLaren: *Funny How We Don't Talk Any More.*

COMMENTATOR: It was never Malcolm McLaren's stunt. Winning the court case went against the Situationist image he prided himself on when he fashioned the pop group he considered his sole creation.

McLAREN: What a drag. How boring. What grates me is that this result makes Branson's Virgin look vaguely 'hip'. I absolutely just feel dreadful about that. If only they'd dragged Mister Pickle off to gaol. Now that would have been brilliant. I would have visited the old hippie in the Scrubs.

COMMENTATOR: But McLaren could not carp at the financial consequences of the ensuing publicity…

McLAREN: Mind you, I must say the album's selling truck loads… literally truck loads.

COMMENTATOR: Branson trumped McLaren as The Trickster.

As Mike Oldfield's 'Tubular Bells' plays:

STORY-TELLER: More than satisfied with Kinsley's performance and the *coup de theatre* he had pulled off in court, Richard Branson presented the Reverend Professor with a copy of *Tubular Bells*.

COMMENTATOR: But the Prof's own musical taste did not stretch as far as 70's Prog.

STORY-TELLER: Kinsley was a fine interpreter of the Border Ballads of his native northern land which he performed in mufti in local folk clubs, to such acclaim that he was oft mistaken as the genuine article: a Caledonian shepherd or a Highland crofter, rather than a distinguished academic from the university. He quickly passed on this uncalled-for and unwelcome gift to one of the young lecturers in the department who might better appreciate its worth. Knowingly or not, Kinsley mis-named the album: 'Tubular Balls'.

COMMENTATOR: A characteristically hyperbolic leader in The Sun…

STORY-TELLER: The old currant bun…

COMMENTATOR: …revealed the extent to which the collective tabloid nose had been put out of joint:

SUN EDITORIAL: Astonishing! Johnny Rotten and his foul-mouthed Sex Pistols have put up two fingers to the world.

STORY-TELLER: Gotcha? 'Fraid not.

COMMENTATOR: And on the following Sunday the verdict was commemorated for posterity in the *Sunday Express* by the cartoonist Giles.

STORY-TELLER: On a rainy city street, with a brutalist office block at the edge of the left margin and buildings of an older England retreating into the right of the frame an ensemble cast of the Great British Public is out on parade. A hunched Old Lady in a flea-blown fur coat is surrounded by a shocked cross-section of the populace, one of whom covers the ears of a uniformed schoolboy. She is reacting to a smirking little girl in a push-chair, propelled by a groovy young mother who provides the words of the caption:

GILES CHARACTER: But Auntie, the Magistrates say it <u>isn't</u> a rude word anymore.

COMMENTATOR: Years later John Mortimer Q.C. remembered…

STORY-TELLER: Mis-remembered!

Does he sound slurred when he makes this recollection?

MORTIMER: I called a lexicographer from Nottingham University who was also a vicar. He gave evidence to the fact that the Word meant the rigging of a medieval man o' war.

STORY-TELLER: What? Frigging in the rigging? Where did that come from? Some socialist champagne had clearly been imbibed.

Mortimer's mis-recollection continues:

MORTIMER: The Sex Pistols were acquitted of that ridiculous charge and that was the last I saw of Mister Rotten... One of the most intelligent young men it's been my privilege to meet.

COMMENTATOR: John Lydon...

STORY-TELLER: Still not yet <u>Lord</u> Johnny Rotten...

COMMENTATOR: ...also had memories of that day.

Some other drink has also possibly been imbibed?

LYDON: Nottingham.... My kind of people. Going around the city was the best pub crawl I've ever been on. Fantastic.

DISSOLVE.

MONTAGE. REDNECK BARS.

Booing, jeering, bottles smashing.

STORY-TELLER: The triumph was short-lived. The Sex Pistols were all but dead already.

COMMENTATOR: Less than two months after the trial, the fractious band embarked on a misbegotten tour of the United States. McLaren had deliberately booked them into Deep South dives where the redneck clientele was guaranteed to be anything but welcoming to English Punk Rockers.

STORY-TELLER: What provocation! Those soixante-huitard Situationists would've been proud.

COMMENTATOR: In San Antonio Texas Sid Vicious…

STORY-TELLER: …ever the exponent of diplomatic rhetoric…

COMMENTATOR: …berated the cowboy audience.

Poor junkie Sid shouts out:

SID VICIOUS: You're a bunch of faggots!

COMMENTATOR: With predictable results.

Bottles smash around Sid.

STORY-TELLER: In Memphis Tennessee Sid went AWOL and was eventually found with this desperate plea carved into his chest:

SID VICIOUS: Gimme a fix!

COMMENTATOR: The swan song took place on January the Fourteenth 1978 in San Francisco at the Winterland Ballroom…

STORY-TELLER: Aptly named. Their closing number was a cover version of Iggy and the Stooges' *No Fun*.

COMMENTATOR: When the song was over, a temporarily defeated Johnny Rotten…

STORY-TELLER: …whom McLaren later dubbed:

McLAREN: The Charles Dickens of rock and roll.

COMMENTATOR: …addressed the crowd:

CUT TO:

INT. WINTERLAND. NIGHT.

The disappointed audience jeer and boo as the band falls apart on No Fun:

LYDON: Ever get the feeling you've been cheated? Good night.

STORY-TELLER: Talking to himself as much as to the let-down paying punters. Never mind.

The final verdict?

COMMENTATOR: An almost-forgotten footnote in the history of the defence of the freedom of expression…

STORY-TELLER: An always-to-be-remembered victory in the history of my home town…

COMMENTATOR: Now, over four decades later, the time is right to assess the cultural significance of…

He cuts her off sharply – enough is enough!

STORY-TELLER: Bollocks!!!

THE END

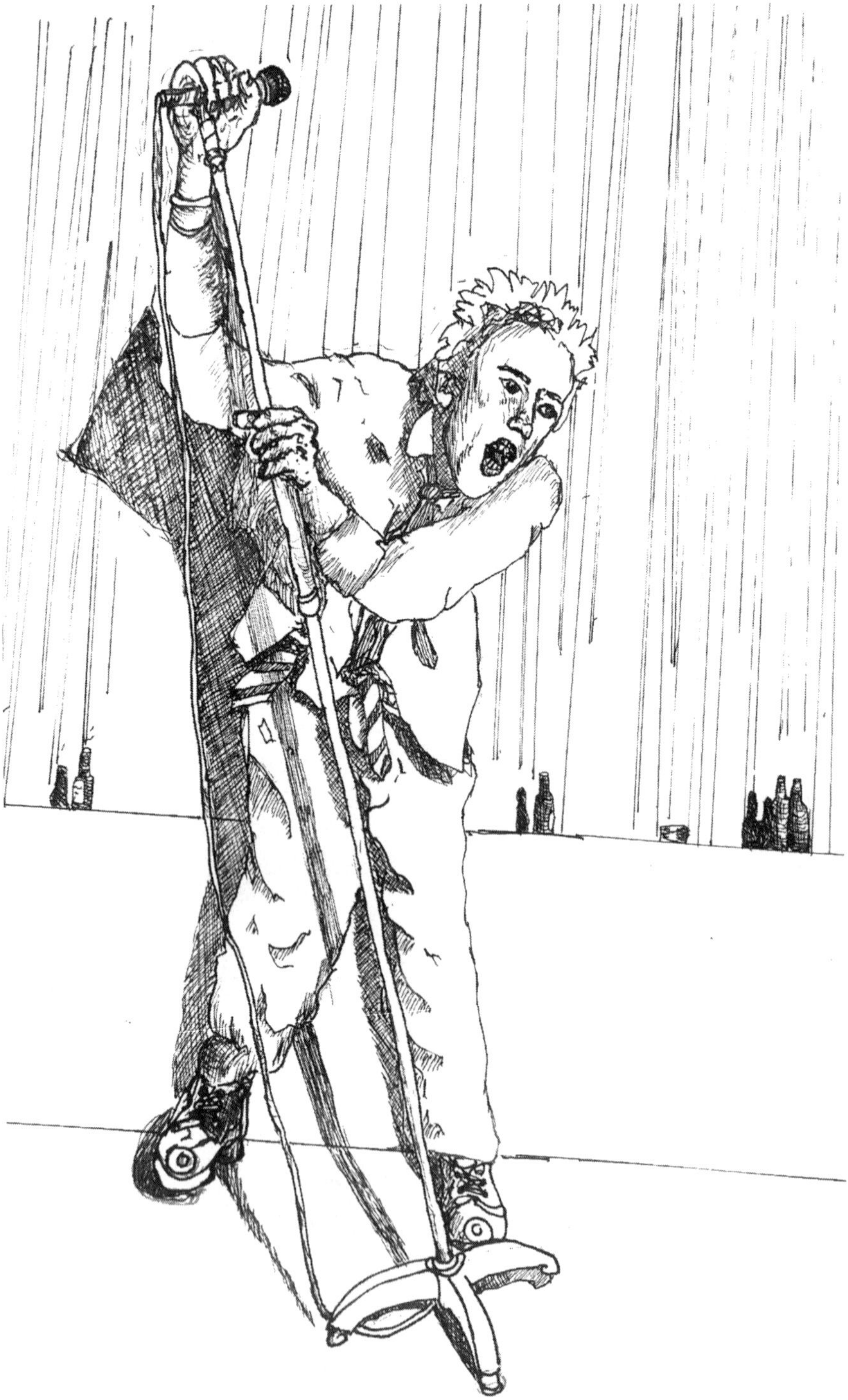

AFTERWORD

I never saw The Sex Pistols. But this is not really about them – it's about my home town. But I was not living in Nottingham in 1977. So I have no experience of the city's first iteration of Virgin Records, which provided the inciting locale for this farcical footnote in the history of freedom of expression. The only first-hand account I've discovered comes from an anonymous blog, *Punk Girl Diaries,* posted in August 2019, a heady evocation of those dear dead days beyond recall:

> *The Virgin Records shop in Nottingham was one of the coolest places I've been to. On the ground floor it was nothing particularly out of the ordinary, but it had a spiral staircase that led down to a really dingy room where punks seemed to hang out the whole time.... we were in awe of the leather-clad boys and girls down there. There's a kind of thrilling fear that you get when you're just a young kid entering this kind of cool den... I felt like I was living the punk dream in that shop.*

A patina of nostalgia settles upon memory. And every crossword solver knows that 'nostalgia' is an anagram for 'lost again'. Nevertheless… 'Hey ho, let's go!'

My own life-spiralling encounter with what would subsequently be labelled 'Punk' was in the Lent Term (yeah, yeah, I know, but honesty is the least worst policy) in the unlikely environs of Magdalene (truthfully pronounced 'maudlin') College, Cambridge. My friend Jon Savage – soon to be the peerless chronicler of the definitive history of the 'movement' *England's Dreaming* – dropped the needle of the arm of his turntable onto the opening track of first album by The Ramones: *Blitzkreig Bop.* All the cobwebs of prog-rock pretension were blown away by this amazing knowingly tongue-in-cheek onslaught. When I rushed out to buy a copy from the city's apparently 'groovy' indie record shop – where *Dark Side Of The Moon* seemed to be on permanent replay – I was sneeringly informed: 'We don't sell that shit.'

At the expense of self-mythologising, I had at around the same time written one of the first ecstatic reviews of Patti Smith's *Horses* – though read by few as it appeared in a student rag. From the 'iconic' – that over-used, mis-applied word but here entirely visually accurate – cover photograph by Robert Mapplethorpe to the first line of *Gloria (In Excelsis Deo)*: 'Jesus died for somebody's sins but not mine…' here was the manifestation of the High-

Priestess, the Delphic oracular mould-breaking wordsmith channelling shamanic, poetic, prophetic passion from Blake, Baudelaire and Rimbaud which she fused to the shape-shifting lineage of pop music idols: Dylan, Hendrix, Morrison, Reed. Patti Smith was the apotheosis of the transformative power of Rock 'n Roll. She took control of that legacy and I was captivated, an acolyte.

Shortly before taking my Finals – as degree exams are terminally nominated as if there is no life thereafter – I hitched down to London to witness her first British concert at the Roundhouse in London in May 1976. And after the results were posted in the eminently vocational discipline of Social Anthropology (Phew! Now what?) I thumbed down again to see The Ramones at the same venue on, aptly enough, the Fourth of July – Independence Day. Attempting to jump on a Routemaster to Chalk Farm, the red bus accelerated and I slipped off the platform to be dragged down the road hanging onto the rail until it stopped at the next set of lights whilst the smirking conductor looked on.

By the time I arrived at the Roundhouse my Levis were ripped at the knees and blood was congealing on my desert boots. Accidentally, unknowingly, I had adopted the appropriate sartorial mode for this historic event.

That night I must have subconsciously come to the decision that fieldwork would be undertaken, not among the Chimbu of Highland New Guinea, but in the wilder locale of Lower Manhattan – at that time the grimy, scary, bankrupt Gotham City of *Taxi Driver* (infamous Daily News headline: 'Ford to City: "Drop Dead" ') rather than the spruce Metropolis of brash Trump Tower and Disneyfied Times Square.

Which is why I missed 'England's Dreaming'.

Somehow, I secured a job under a variety of aliases and cobbled-together social security numbers (has the Statute of Limitations elapsed or should I plead the Fifth Amendment?) in Market Research. If Don Draper from *Mad Men* was at the top of the totem pole imagine the likes of us at the bottom of the pile pre-computer coding responses to cat flea collars. Nevertheless, I found myself working with the most fascinating, talented, bizarre bunch of bananas, none of whom foresaw their future in this office on Forty First Street – one block from stardom. This was still the epoch of two Bloody Mary breakfasts and three Martini lunches – not, mind you, in the Oak Room of the Plaza Hotel ('a most unusual day', check out *North By Northwest*) but in The Blarney Stone round the corner.

After-hours hangout was a dive on the Bowery: CBGB. Not that any of the habitués knew that these gnomic initials stood for the kind of sounds loved by the legendary owner, Hilly Kristal: *Country Blue Grass Blues*. Such down homey folksy fiddling was always going to be a non-starter in grungy downtown Manhattan where skid-row sidewalks were bejewelled with shards of broken green liquor bottles shining like fugazy emeralds in the late afternoon sun and where the dazed denizens of the Palace Hotel next door to the venue, where Bobby Fuller of *I Fought The Law And The Law Won* fame was reputed to have breathed his last, stumbled over nodding junkies and crashed-out winos whose pavements were their pillows. Undeterred, Hilly added: OMFUG: *Other Music for Uplifting Gourmandizers*!

The shocking ambience of Lionel Rogosin's 1956 ground-breaking cine-verité film *On The Bowery* had not yet been erased, though the Third Avenue elevated railway had long since been demolished. In bars which could have provided the set design for Eugene O'Neill's pipe-dream masterpiece *The Ice Man Cometh* shots of Wild Irish Rose whiskey could be purchased for a quarter slapped down on the counter served up with that small yet fatal glass of beer to chase down the real drink – it continues to pain me whenever topers on this side of the pond insist on 'a whisky chaser'. William S. Burroughs lived here in his securely bolted and well-armed Bunker and could be seen on *noli me tangere* occasions in immaculate three-piece tailoring, improbable in this context.

CBGB had evolved into the home of the 'New Wave', featuring the very bands I'd come to NYC to follow, in an intimate space where aficionados could stand up close and personal to watch the magnificent Tom Verlaine, every bit as romantic as his namesake, falling into the arms of Venus de Milo and punch the air with Patti as she urged: 'Go Rimbaud, Go Rimbaud, Go Rimbaud and Go Johnny Go.' (Arthur of that ilk, not Sly Stallone – though who really knew?)

What was that anagram of nostalgia?

Having decided, doubtless without much more consideration than the decision which took me there in the first instance, that post-structuralism beckoned after all, I left NYC on August the Sixteenth, 1977. A date never to be forgotten. When I boarded the red-eye at JFK Elvis Presley was still, though barely, alive at Graceland, Memphis Tennessee. By the time I cleared customs at Heathrow the following morning the headlines were blaring: 'The King Is Dead'.

Cornered for a soundbite in Tokyo airport John Lennon spitefully muttered: *Elvis died when he went into the army. That's when they killed him. That's when they castrated him. The rest of it was just a living death.* With unfeeling sociopathy, Malcolm McLaren gave his vindictive opinion: *Too bad it couldn't have been Mick Jagger.* Even more tersely, and with characteristic eloquence, the recently appointed bassist of the Sex Pistols, one Sid Vicious, gobbed out: *Elvis was dead before he died.* It was given to a Graceland spokesperson to pronounce the official verdict: *Mister Presley's terminal event was experienced on the commode.*

Le Roi est mort! Vive… Qui?

On the front page splash from the New York *Daily News* Elvis trumps David Berkowitz. For this was, let us not forget, The Summer of the Son of Sam.

Back in England, with a suspicion that I'd already missed the boat, I went to check out the apparent home of Punk in London, The Roxy in Covent Garden, to be not a little shocked. Many New York musicians rightly blanched at this label now indiscriminately stuck to such diverse bands over there. 'Punk' was an epithet given to good-looking juvenile delinquents banged up on Rikers Island for the salacious delectation of older crims in return for small favours.

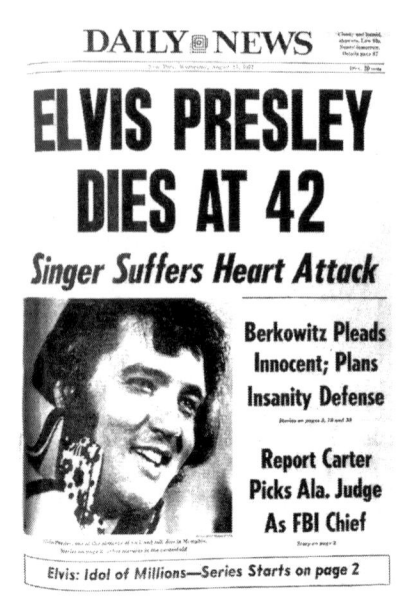

The difference between those CBGB outfits and their younger UK counterparts was that those Yanks really knew what to do with their instruments. No-one could accuse Television of being three-chord wonders. The grungy pose of The Ramones was always an art-work in inverted commas. Pogo to Blondie? Gob at David Byrne? Not in New York, where, as Jonathan Richman reminded us: 'Pablo Picasso never got called an asshole'.

But those adolescent London punks possessed, it must be said, a much more developed fashion sense than their transatlantic equivalents. On the Bowery and in the East Village college drop-out wannabee intellectuals were slumming it in unwashed personalised t-shirts, ersatz biker jackets and ripped denims with well-thumbed if unread books of poetry sticking out of the back pockets. Johnny Rotten despised the New York look for obvious reasons – he was far too original a thinker and dresser. Sartorially over here, this style signalled a complete break, a paradigm shift from what had gone before in teenage clothing. The London contingent, male, female and whatever in between, were home-made heroic, DIY provocative, colourfully splayed out against monochrome skies as they legged it away from bicycle-chain swinging Teds and truncheon-wielding Mets.

In Noo Yawk the collective eyelid seemed hardly to have been batted by this 'new sociological phenomenon'. There were far too many competing freakshows on the quotidian Manhattan Midway. Ground-breaking tracks were rarely played on FM radio (oh, that Fleetwood Mac; oh, those Eagles); the few available discs barely shifted any significant units; the downtown clubs and bars were no bigger than the average suburban garage – where many of those bands had presumably started. But in hypocritical blackout Merrie Engerland those few brave souls striving to escape the straitjacket of No Future conformity had been caricatured and demonised as tabloid Folk Devils, provoking what sociologists label a 'Moral Panic'.

Punk in England was political. A far more serious game was afoot.

The antediluvian legislation dusted off the statute book to censor *Never Mind The Bollocks* was mobilised in June 1899 – not as it transpired to curtail lavatorial flyers but to stymie salacious posters for a celebrated female artiste whose act, perforce, necessitated scant clothing. In a House of Commons debate one John Kelly, Conservative member for Camberwell North, tabled a question to the then Home Secretary, Henry Matthews:

> *I beg to ask the Secretary of State for the Home Department whether his attention has been called to the advertisement of the female aerialist known as 'Zaeo', performing at the London Aquarium which is more or less indecent and ought not to be exhibited…*
> *The proper course would be for the Police Authorities to take action under the Indecent Advertisements Act of 1889.*

Though, in retrospect, there was more than a hint of masculine scopophilia involved, the Home Secretary gave his considered deliberation: *The matter should be allowed to drop*. Zaeo's controversial aerial contortions were allowed to continue.

But seventy-eight years later the 'matter' would not be 'dropped' for another tenuous tribunal for even more destabilising performers. Thus it was that in November 1977 a one-act comedy, which could easily have had a tragic result, would be played out in Courtroom Three of the Guildhall in my home town.

As someone who has worked in the disputed genre of 'drama-documentary' I was liberated to discover that Magistrates Courts do not take verbatim transcripts of their hearings. I had been granted the latitude to make it up! Albeit securely based on contemporary press coverage (somewhat limited) and personal recollections (even more so).

Everything is True. Only the Facts have been Changed in the Interests of Drama. When Truth Becomes Legend Print The Legend.

I'd been fortunate to meet the great John Mortimer on a couple of occasions – literary not legal I hasten to add – but had never asked him about this case which, anyway, he later completely misremembered. He died in 2009.

Chief expert witness for the Defence James Kinsley (not Kingsley as so often erroneously reported) was also long gone, though his reputation continues to cast a shadow. For young jazzy pedagogues in his department he was an old-fashioned laughing stock, parading around the campus in clerical garb and performing border ballads in folk clubs with a finger in his ear. Seeking scandal about their unloved Head of Department, Prof. Kinsley was purported to have a Secret Life as an habitué of a seedy flea-pit on Milton Street, the well-remembered *Moulin Rouge*, with its sporadically flashing neon windmill vainly conjuring up a simulacrum in the far-flung East Midlands of the exotic Parisian Pigalle original. The respected academic's ventures into the cinematic underworld caused his sniggering underlings to consider him as one of what was then called the 'dirty mac brigade.' Objection, Your Worship! Such a judgment may be entirely unwarranted. For this was the only commercial cinema in town which screened European art movies. Granted, they were shown alongside what passed in such prurient times as 'adult entertainment'. Not unusual to find double bills of healthy and efficient nudist camp 'documentaries' such as *Naked As Nature Intended* coupled with Fellini's *8 ½*. (His 'hat size' according to rag and bone man Albert Steptoe – another unlikely template for Johnny Rotten's stage persona). I'm not ashamed to say that I received a significant portion of my own cinephiliac education perched on those sticky velveteen seats. I was there for the Antonioni and the Bergman. Honest. Though I confess remaining goggle-eyed through Harrison Marks's oeuvre.

Sir Richard Branson was contacted, via an intermediary, about his central role in this tale and I was rather chuffed when he willingly accepted my request to share his memories. I had been due to receive a call from his lair in the British Virgin Islands in late March 2020… but then the virus struck and the world went into lockdown. Any subsequent communication remains in a state of post-viral postponement. An irritation of forty-three years ago, however significant then, must hardly be at the top of his agenda now. These days the ambitions of 'Britain's Best-Loved Businessman' (sic) are extra-terrestrial.

Every effort was made to touch base with Chris Seale (not Searle, yet another frequently misrepresented nomination). He was the initial performer in this circus, unsung and side-lined as the potential fall-guy whose name was on the charge sheet, who stood in the dock to plead Not Guilty and whose reputation could have taken a plunge had the verdict gone another way. Unfortunately, we never managed to secure trans-hemispheric communication, which I much regret.

So the only one of the central players in the trial I have been privileged to meet has been Caroline Coon. She admitted that her memories of the incident were something of a blur – not because it was so long ago or that so much else was happening in her busy life at that time – but because, which I hadn't quite clocked, it was all over in a flash. Fortunately, her examination by Mortimer as to the significance of the music and the maliciousness of this prosecution as well as her successful sparring match with Prosecutor David Ritchie were well-covered in the most complete account of the process from the time in a New Musical Express article by Ross Stapleton.

What did this squall in a half-pint pot amount to? Surely not a Nightmare, more of a Daydream on King Street? What does this incident signify forty years on when afar and asunder? Was it just a public-school stunt as dismissed by manager McLaren and artist Jamie Reid, whose tossed-off album cover is now rightly lauded as an exemplar of twentieth-century design? Or does this half-forgotten event serve as a reminder to be forever vigilant against attacks, however seemingly trivial, which would curtail artistic license?

All Together Now, to the tune of 'Colonel Bogey': Bollocks! And the same to you! (Repeat *ad infinitum* as long as necessary).

ABOUT THE AUTHOR

Michael Eaton is a Nottingham-based dramatist for cinema, television, radio and the theatre who has written TV docu-dramas such as *Why Lockerbie?*; the BAFTA nominated *Shoot to Kill*, and *Shipman* for ITV as well as original dramas including *Signs and Wonders* and *Flowers Of The Forest* for the BBC. His script for the HBO feature film *Fellow Traveller* won Best Screenplay at the British Film Awards in 1989. He has written four plays for Nottingham Playhouse of which the last was *Charlie Peace – His Amazing Life and Astounding Legend*, also the subject of his 2017 publication for Five Leaves. He has adapted several works of Charles Dickens for BBC Radio 4 including *The Pickwick Papers* starring Timothy Spall; the little-known *George Silverman's Explanation* with Paul Scofield; the ghost story *The Bride's Chamber*, and *The Special Correspondent for Posterity*, based on Dickens's journalism and letters, which was commissioned for the Dickens bicentenary of 2012 for which he also co-wrote and narrated an Arena documentary *Dickens and Film* and co-curated a three-month retrospective of Dickens cinematic adaptations at the *bfi* Southbank. His theatrical version of *Great Expectations*, which featured Jane Asher as Miss Havisham, premiered at the West Yorkshire Playhouse in 2016. Other original radio plays include *Washington 9/11*; *The Conflict Is Over*, about the Northern Ireland peace process; *Out of the Blue*; *By A Young Officer – Churchill on the North-West Frontier* and, with the composer Neil Brand, *The Cave of Harmony* and *Waves Breaking On A Shore*. His latest radio plays are *Never Mind The Ballocks* (sic), a shorter version of the present publication, and *A Grain of Wheat*, an adaptation of the 1967 novel by the great Kenyan writer Ngũgĩ wa Thiong'o. His adaptation of Agatha Christie's *Murder On The Orient Express* for Audible was the winner of the first Cameo Book-to-Audio award in 2018. He was a Senior Scholar at King's College, Cambridge where he studied Social Anthropology and, thirty-five years later, made *The Masks of Mer*, a documentary film about the anthropologist Alfred Haddon, distributed by the Royal Anthropological Institute and the subject of his 2015 BBC Radio 3 drama *Head Hunters*. The text of this, together with a well-illustrated introduction, was published by Shoestring Press, publisher of his well-received translation of Ernest Renan's play *The Priest of Nemi*, which also includes an essay about the influence of this neglected French drama on J. G. Frazer's *The Golden Bough*, and in 2020 *Based On A True Story*, a collection of essays, monologues and dramas. He was awarded the M.B.E. for Services to Film in the 1999 New Year's honours list and was Visiting Professor in the School of Creative Writing at Nottingham Trent University for which institution he wrote a play, *All Schools Should Be Art Schools*, to commemorate the 170th anniversary of the foundation of the Nottingham School of Art. He received a Doctorate of Letters from NTU in 2020.